Essential Advanced Scales

Electric Bass

Modes of the Melodic Minor, Harmonic Minor, Diminished, Whole-Tone, and Blues Scales

by **Max Palermo**

This book is dedicated to my family.

Project Manager: **Aaron Stang**
Production Coordinator: **Karl Bork**
Art Design: **Carmen Fortunato**

WARNER BROS. PUBLICATIONS
Warner Music Group
An AOL Time Warner Company
USA: 15800 NW 48th Avenue, Miami, FL 33014

IMP
INTERNATIONAL MUSIC PUBLICATIONS LIMITED

ENGLAND: GRIFFIN HOUSE,
161 HAMMERSMITH ROAD, LONDON W6 8BS

C*ontents*

Introduction

The aim of this publication is to provide students of all levels a simple and quick reference guide to the wide-ranging and complex topic of *scales and modes*.

In each chapter you will find an introductory chart explaining the structure and theory of the scale in question, as well as its practical application. The development of the scales in all the keys follows, together with the fingering and tablature for 4 and 5-string basses.

Acquainting yourself with using the scales is an important goal to reach. When used correctly, scales complement the harmonic structure of a piece of music and increase the choice of different sounds, enriching these sounds with new and diverse nuances.

I would therefore advise you to pause after each chapter, taking the time to absorb all the information contained within it. Repeat the scales with a metronome (or a drum machine) and then at the end try and make up your own riffs, both in isolation and as part of a bass line; always keeping the chords of reference in mind.

As these scales are used a lot in different types of music (jazz, fusion, funk, rock...) you will have at your disposal a personal repertoire of patterns that you can use in different harmonic progressions.

Enjoy your work!

The MELODIC MINOR Family

The Melodic Minor Scale

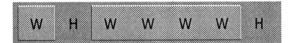

Melodic Minor scale (Jazz Minor scale)

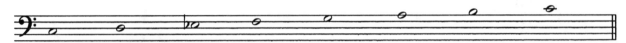

C Melodic Minor (construction)

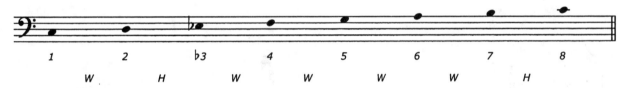

1	2	b3	4	5	6	7	8
W		H	W	W	W	W	H

One octave scale

Chords

Cm   Cm⁶   Cm⁶/₉   Cm(ma7)

2 Octaves

C Melodic Minor (Jazz Minor)

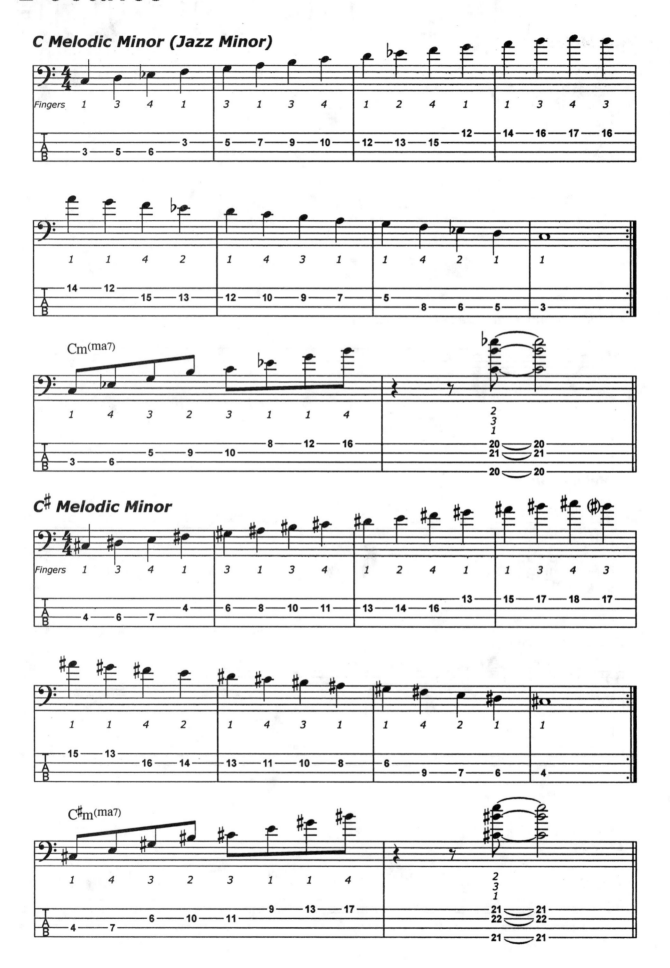

C♯ Melodic Minor

6

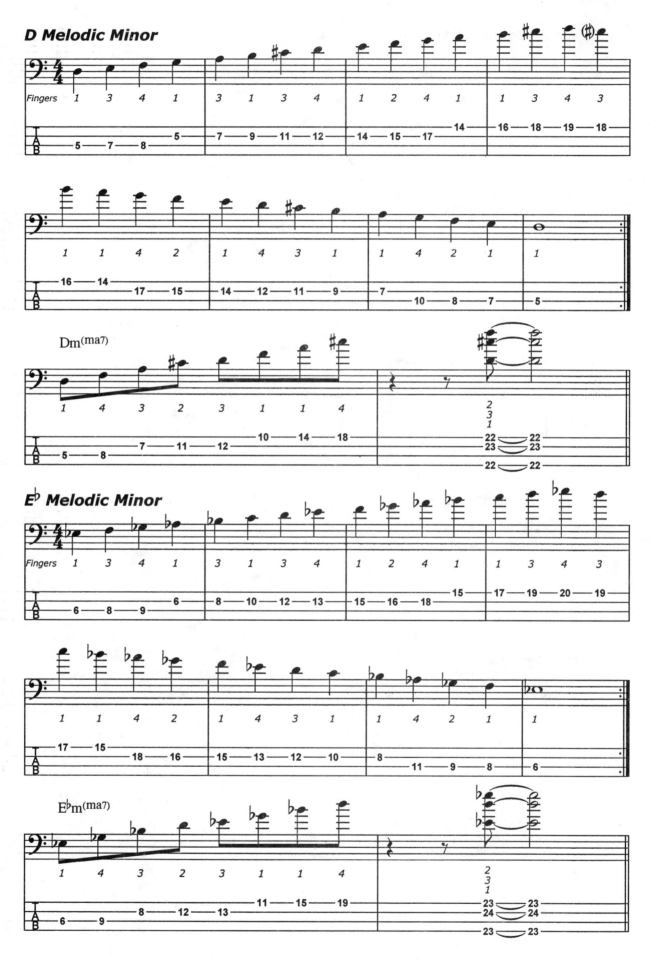

2 Octaves

E Melodic Minor

Em(ma7)

F Melodic Minor

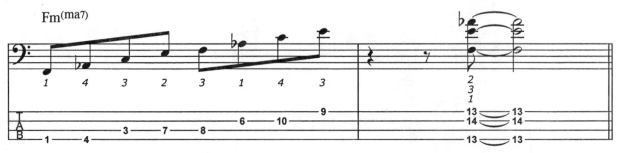

Fm(ma7)

8

F♯ Melodic Minor

F♯m(ma7)

G Melodic Minor

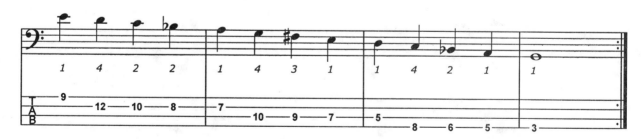

Gm(ma7)

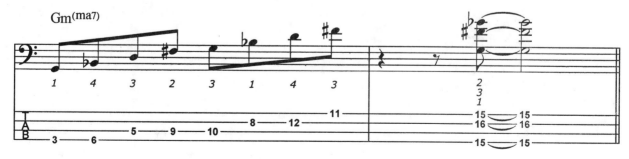

2 Octaves

A♭ Melodic Minor

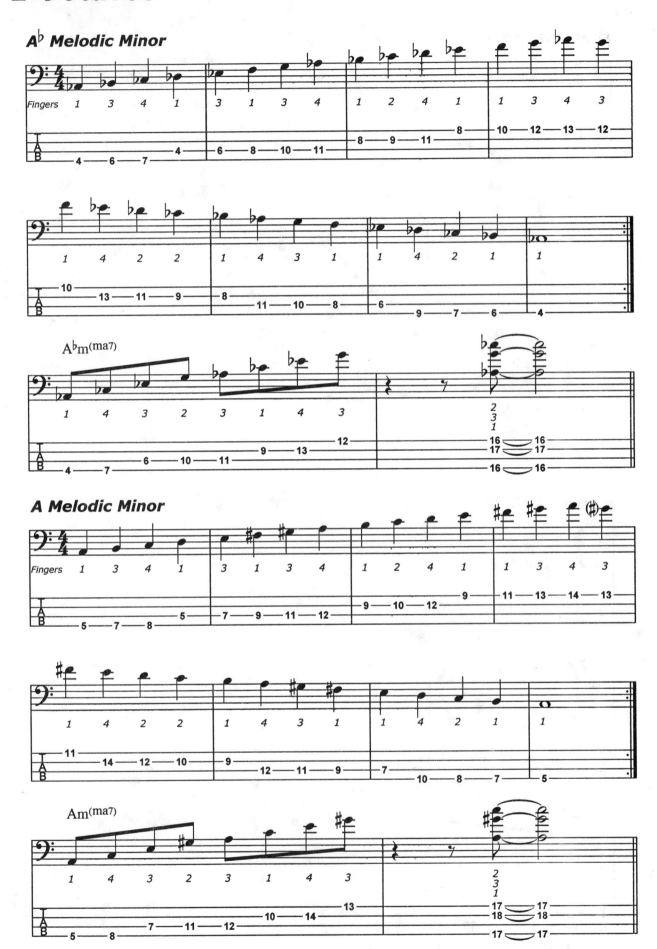

A Melodic Minor

10

B♭ Melodic Minor

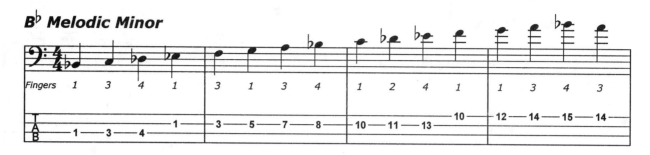

B♭m(ma7)

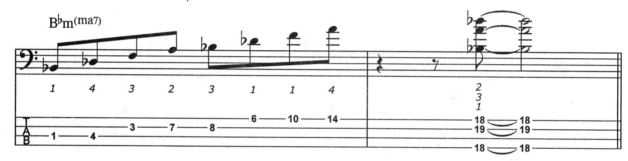

B Melodic Minor

Bm(ma7)

3 Octaves

B Melodic Minor

C Melodic Minor

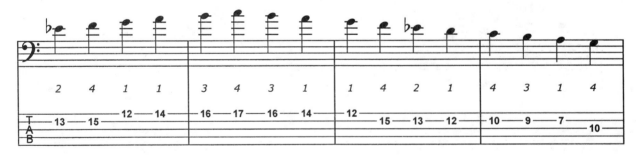

D Melodic Minor

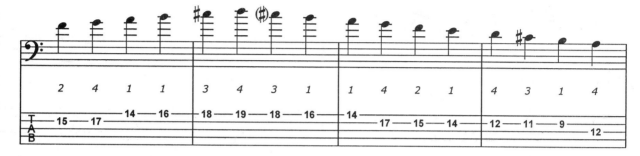

E Melodic Minor

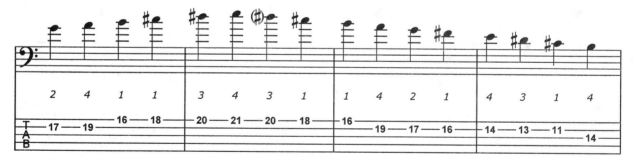

The Dorian ♭2 Mode

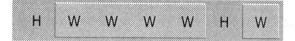

Melodic Minor scale

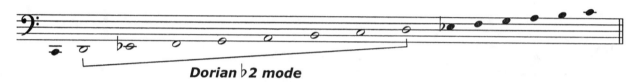

Dorian ♭2 mode

C Dorian ♭2 (construction)

1	♭2	♭3	4	5	6	♭7	8
H	W	W	W	W	H	W	

One octave scale

Chords

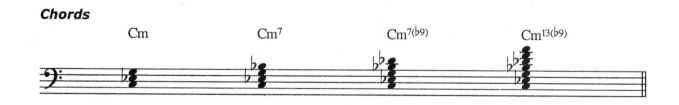

Cm   Cm⁷   Cm⁷⁽♭⁹⁾   Cm¹³⁽♭⁹⁾

2 Octaves

C Dorian ♭2

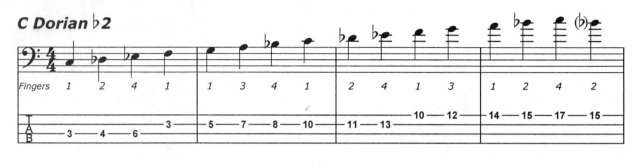

Fingers 1 2 4 1 1 3 4 1 2 4 1 3 1 2 4 2

1 1 4 2 2 1 4 3 1 4 2 2 1

Cm⁷

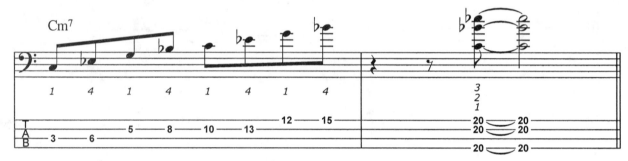

1 4 1 4 1 4 1 4

C♯ Dorian ♭2

Fingers 1 2 4 1 1 3 4 1 2 4 1 3 1 2 4 2

1 1 4 2 2 1 4 3 1 4 2 2 1

C♯m⁷

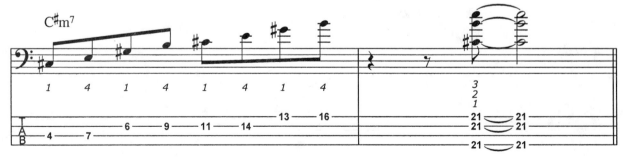

1 4 1 4 1 4 1 4

D Dorian ♭2

Dm⁷

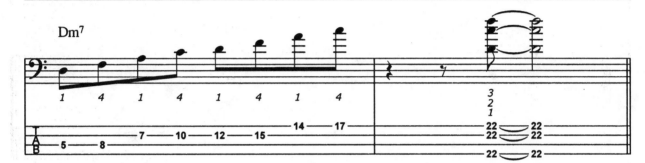

E♭ Dorian ♭2

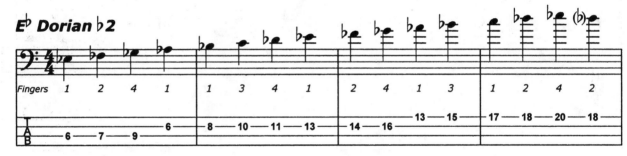

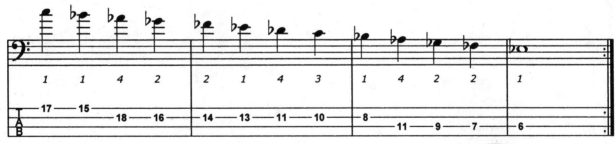

E♭m⁷

E Dorian ♭2

Em⁷

F Dorian ♭2

Fm⁷

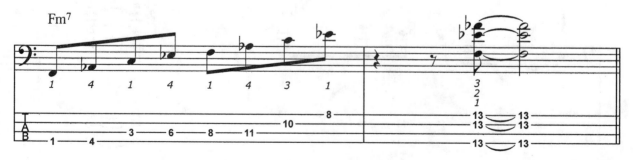

F♯ Dorian ♭2

F♯m⁷

G Dorian ♭2

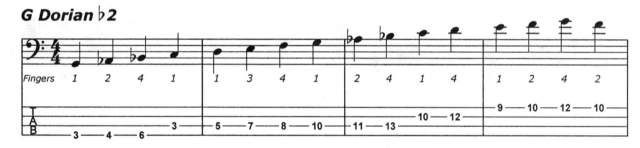

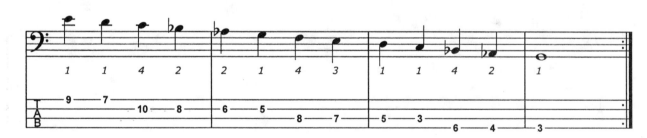

Gm⁷

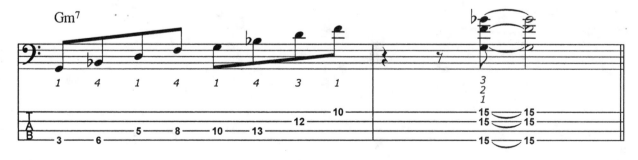

2 Octaves

G♯ Dorian ♭2

A Dorian ♭2

G♯m⁷

Am⁷

20

B♭ Dorian ♭2

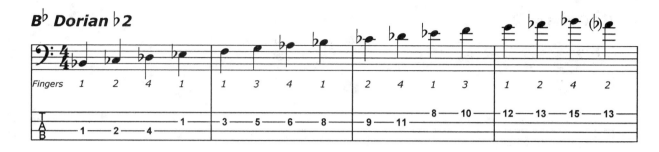

B♭m⁷

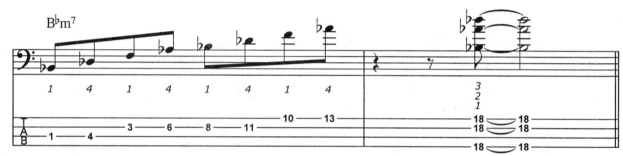

B Dorian ♭2

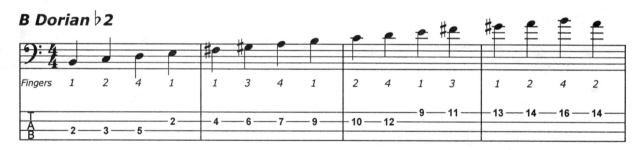

Bm⁷

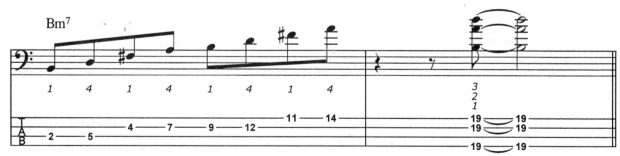

3 Octaves

B Dorian ♭2

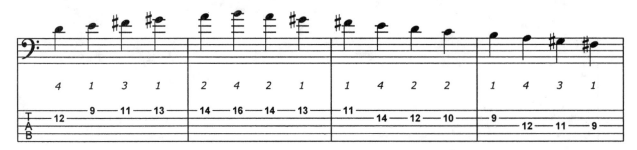

C Dorian ♭2

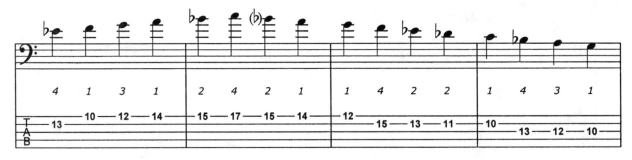

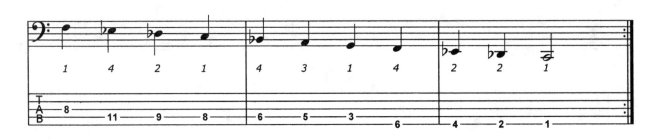

Dorian ♭2 Mode

D Dorian ♭2

E Dorian ♭2

The Lydian Augmented Mode

W	W	W	W	H	W	H

Melodic Minor scale

Lydian Augmented mode

C Lydian Augmented (construction)

1	2	3	#4	#5	6	7	8
W	W	W	W	H	W	H	

One octave scale

Fingers 2   4   1   1   3   4   1   2

Chords

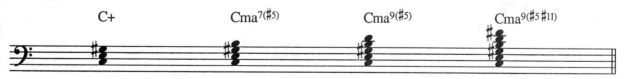

C+   Cma7(#5)   Cma9(#5)   Cma9(#5#11)

2 Octaves

C Lydian Augmented

D♭ Lydian Augmented

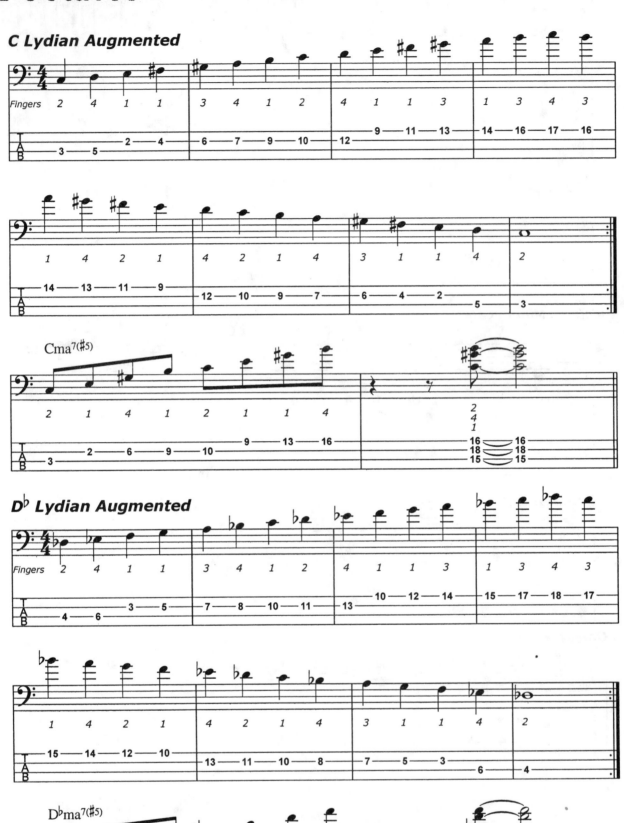

26

D Lydian Augmented

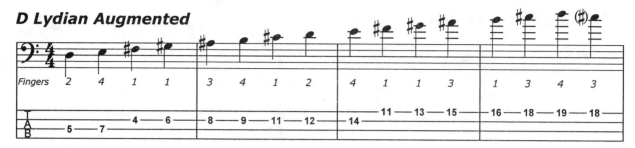

Dma⁷(♯5)

E♭ Lydian Augmented

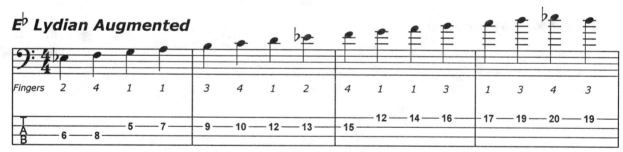

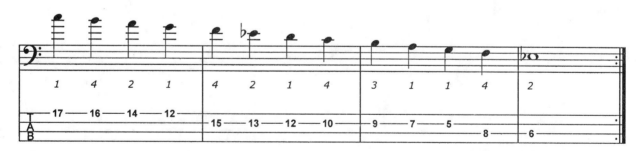

E♭ma⁷(♯5)

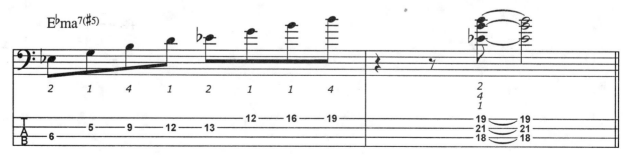

E Lydian Augmented

Ema7(♯5)

F Lydian Augmented

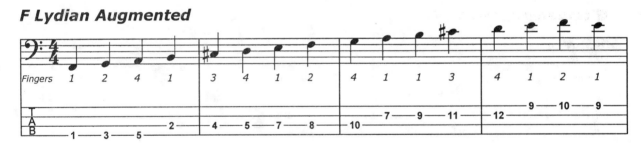

Fma7(♯5)

G♭ Lydian Augmented

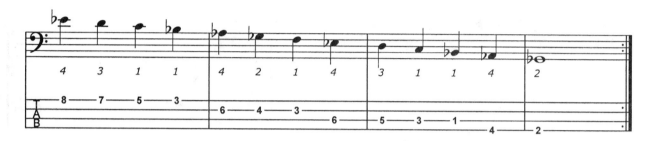

G♭ma⁷⁽♯⁵⁾

G Lydian Augmented

Gma⁷⁽♯⁵⁾

2 Octaves

A♭ Lydian Augmented

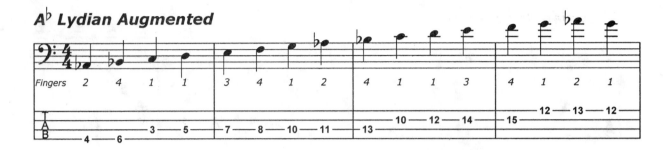

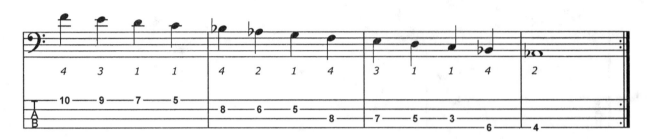

A♭ma7(#5)

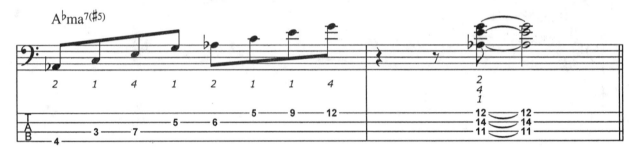

A Lydian Augmented

Ama7(#5)

B♭ Lydian Augmented

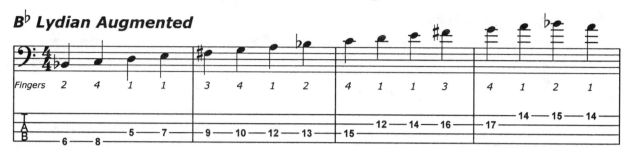

B♭ma7(#5)

B Lydian Augmented

Bma7(#5)

3 Octaves

B Lydian Augmented

C Lydian Augmented

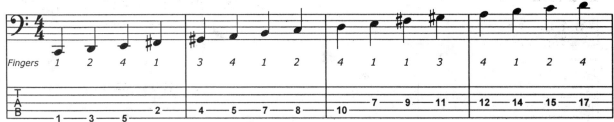

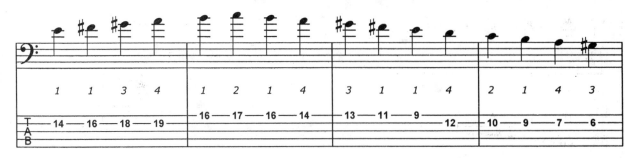

D Lydian Augmented

E Lydian Augmented

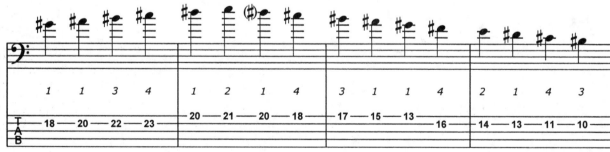

The Lydian Dominant Mode

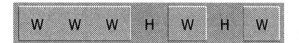

Melodic Minor scale

Lydian Dominant mode

C Lydian Dominant (construction)

1	2	3	#4	5	6	b7	8
W	W	W	H	W	H	W	

One octave scale

Chords

C Lydian Dominant

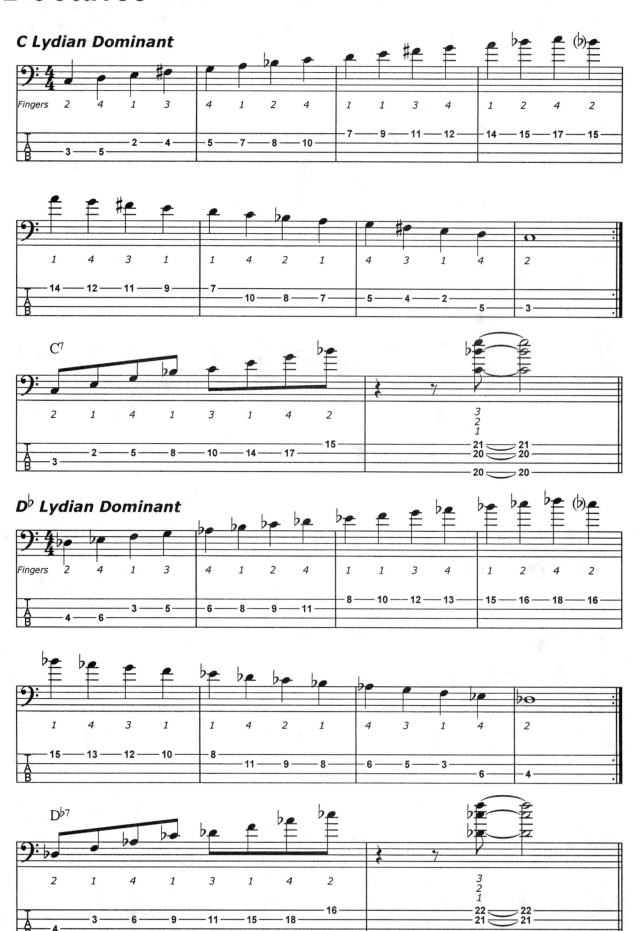

D Lydian Dominant

E♭ Lydian Dominant

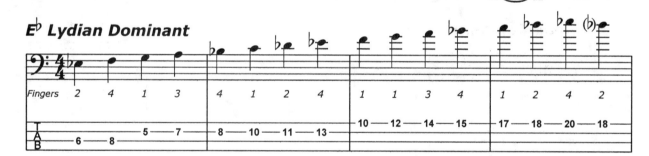

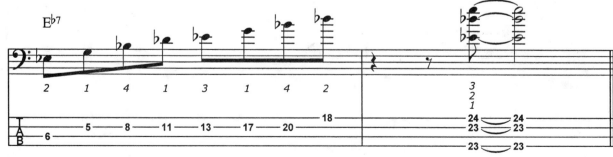

2 Octaves

E Lydian Dominant

F Lydian Dominant

F# Lydian Dominant

F#7

G Lydian Dominant

G7

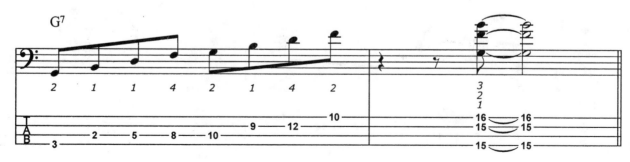

2 Octaves

A♭ Lydian Dominant

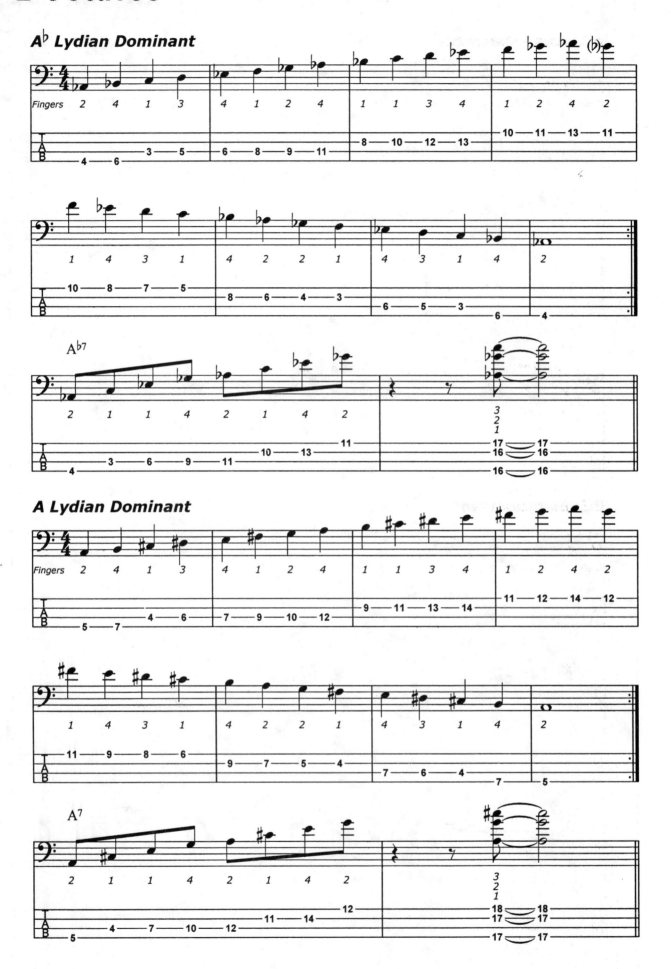

A Lydian Dominant

B♭ Lydian Dominant

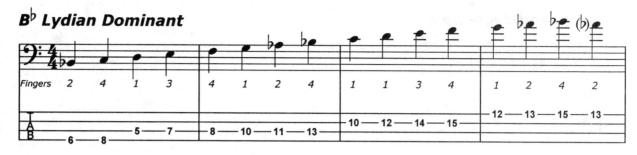

B Lydian Dominant

3 Octaves

B Lydian Dominant

C Lydian Dominant

D Lydian Dominant

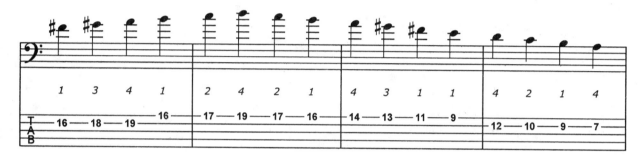

E Lydian Dominant

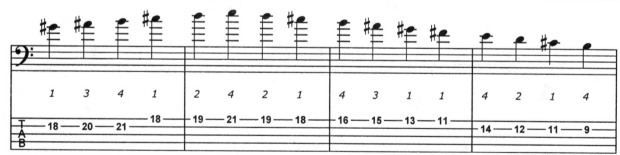

The Mixolydian ♭6 Mode

Melodic Minor scale

Mixolydian ♭6 mode

C Mixolydian ♭6 (construction)

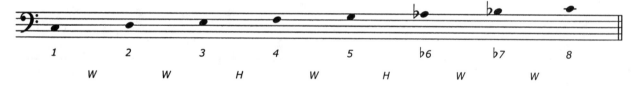

1	2	3	4	5	♭6	♭7	8
W	W	H	W	H	W	W	

One octave scale

Fingers 2   4   1   1   3   4   1   3

Chords

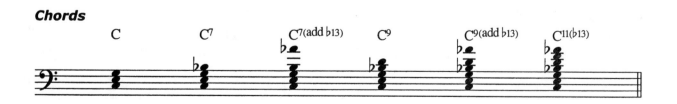

C   C⁷   C⁷(add ♭13)   C⁹   C⁹(add ♭13)   C¹¹(♭13)

2 Octaves

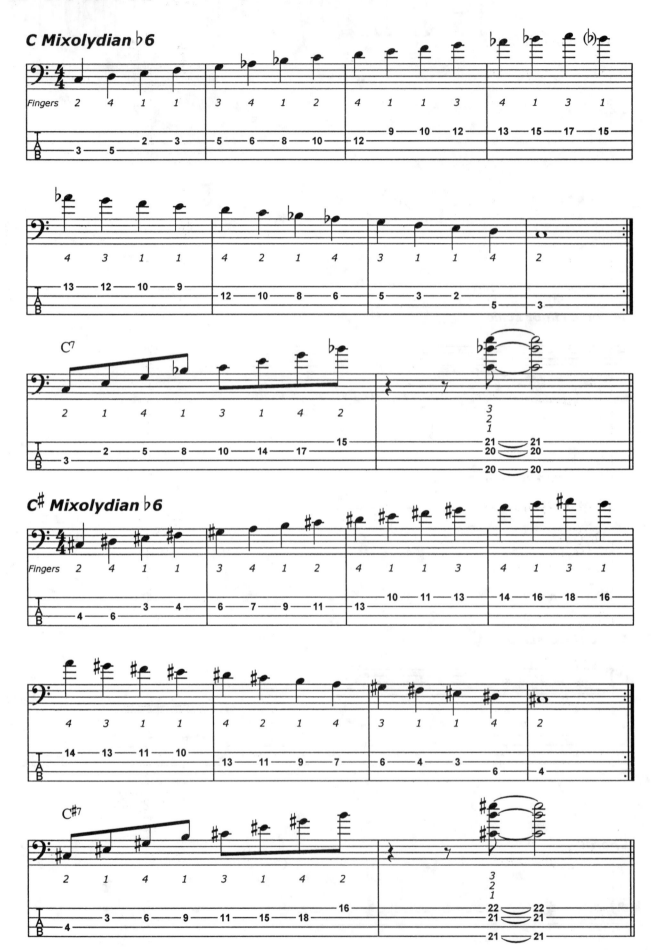

Mixolydian ♭6 Mode

D Mixolydian ♭6

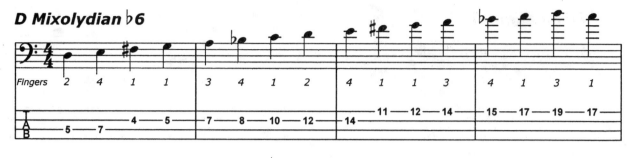

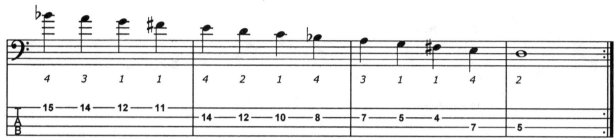

D⁷

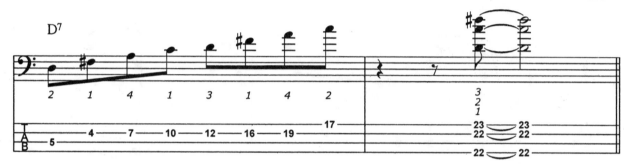

E♭ Mixolydian ♭6

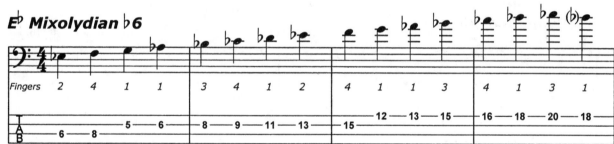

E♭⁷

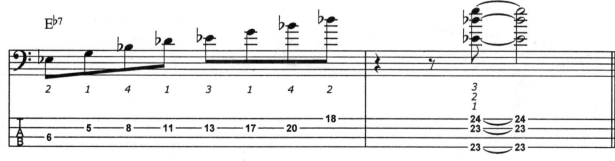

2 Octaves

E Mixolydian ♭6

F Mixolydian ♭6

F# Mixolydian ♭6

F#7

G Mixolydian ♭6

G7

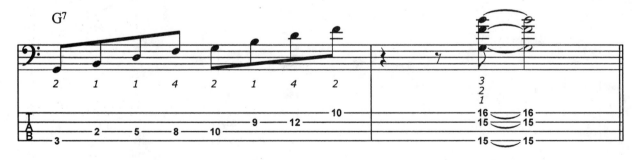

2 Octaves

A♭ Mixolydian ♭6

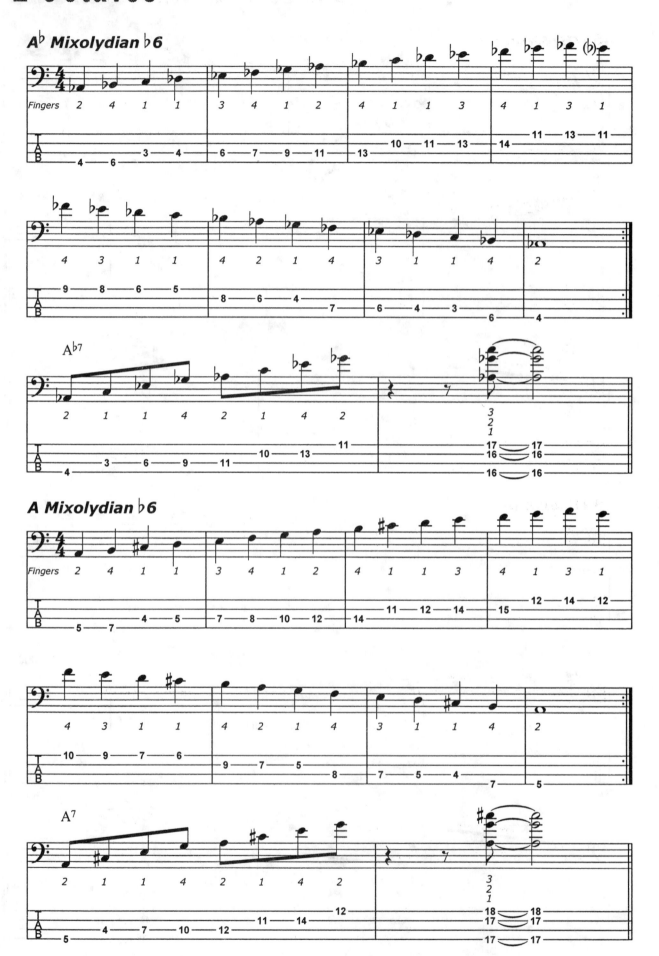

A♭7

A Mixolydian ♭6

A7

Mixolydian ♭6 Mode

B♭ Mixolydian ♭6

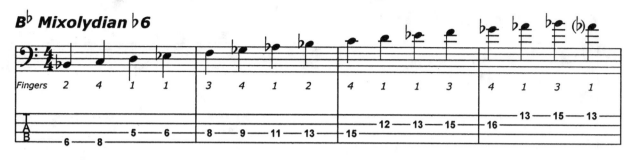

B Mixolydian ♭6

51

3 Octaves

B Mixolydian ♭6

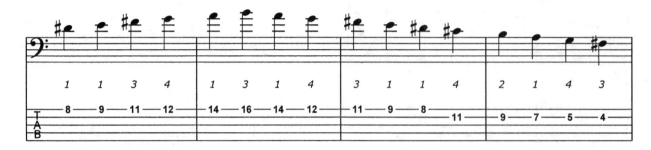

C Mixolydian ♭6

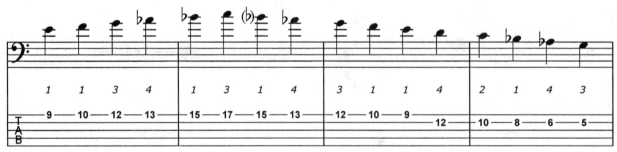

D Mixolydian ♭6

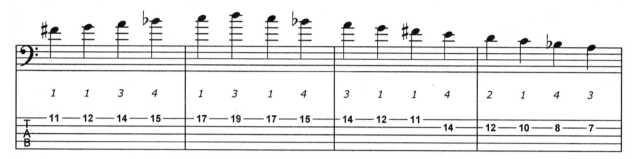

E Mixolydian ♭6

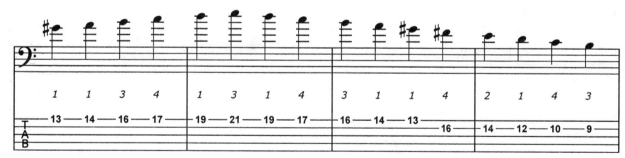

The Locrian ♮2 Mode

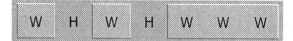

Melodic Minor scale

Locrian ♮2 mode

C Locrian ♮2 (construction)

1	2	♭3	4	♭5	♭6	♭7	8
W	H	W	H	W	W	W	

One octave scale

Fingers   1   3   4   1   2   4   1   3

Chords

C°   Cm7(♭5)   Cm9(♭5)   Cm11(♭5)

2 Octaves

C Locrian ♮2

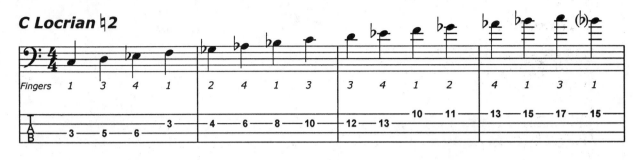

Cm⁷⁽ᵇ⁵⁾

C# Locrian ♮2

C#m⁷⁽ᵇ⁵⁾

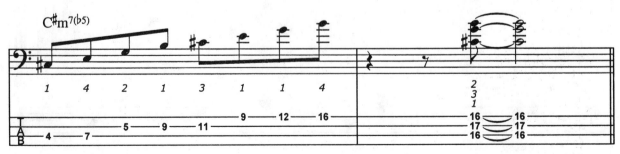

D Locrian ♮2

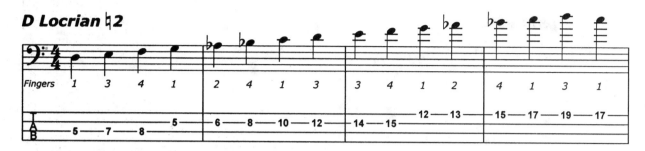

Dm7(♭5)

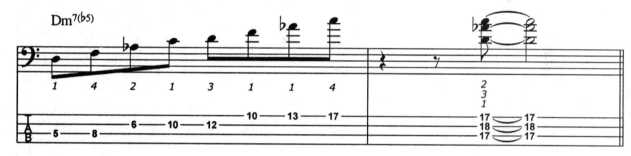

D♯ Locrian ♮2

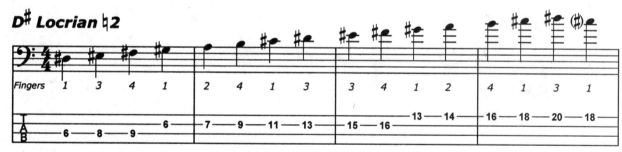

D♯m7(♭5)

2 Octaves

E Locrian ♮2

Fingers

Em7(♭5)

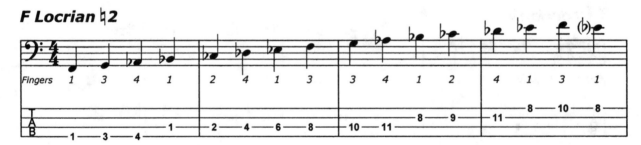

F Locrian ♮2

Fingers

Fm7(♭5)

F# Locrian ♮2

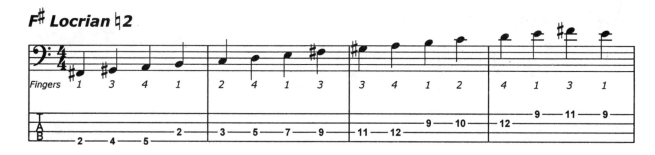

F#m⁷⁽♭⁵⁾

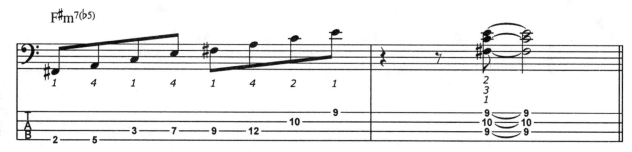

G Locrian ♮2

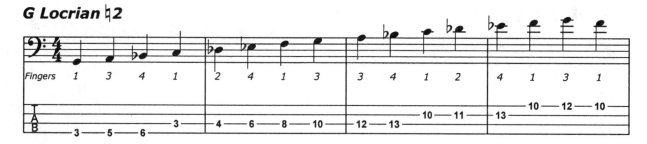

Gm⁷⁽♭⁵⁾

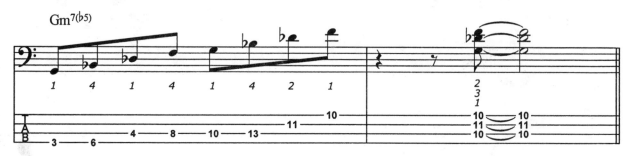

2 Octaves

G# Locrian ♮2

A Locrian ♮2

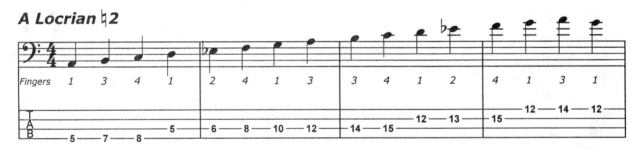

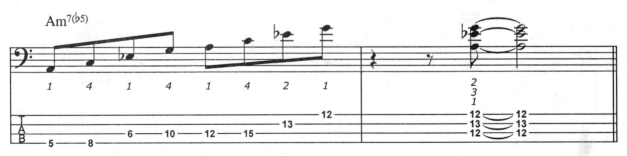

A♯ Locrian ♮2

A♯m7(♭5)

B Locrian ♮2

Bm7(♭5)

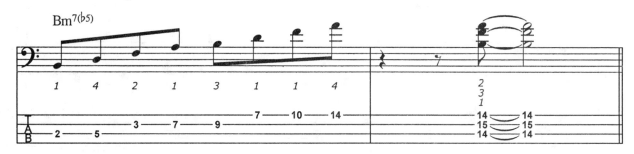

3 Octaves

B Locrian ♮2

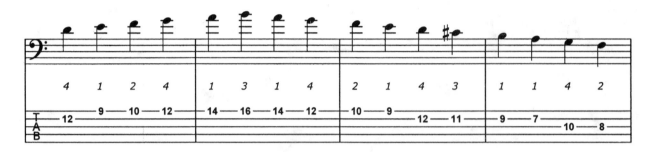

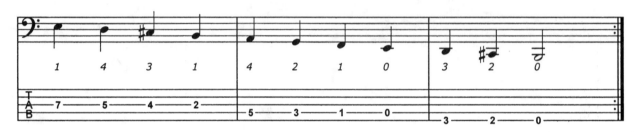

C Locrian ♮2

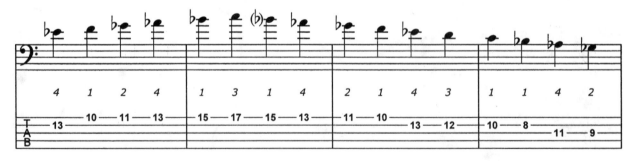

D Locrian ♮2

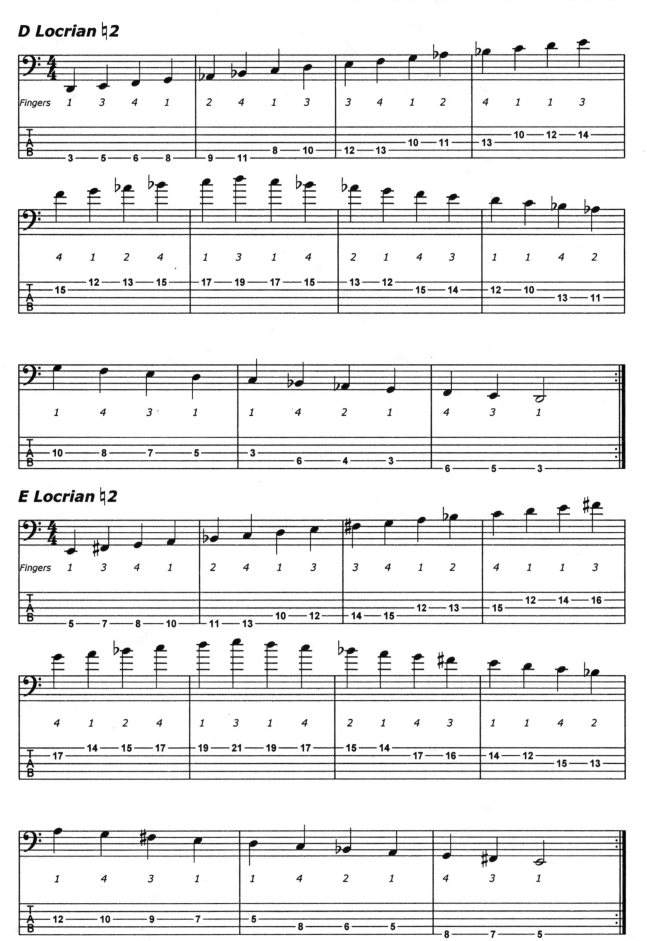

E Locrian ♮2

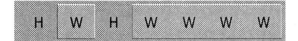

Melodic Minor scale

Altered mode

C Altered (construction)

1	♭2	♭3	♭4 (3)	♭5	♭6	♭7	8
H		W	H	W	W	W	

One octave scale

Chords

C+   C(♭5)   Cm7(♭5)   C7(♯5)   C7(♭5)   C7(♯5♭9)   C7(♭5♯9)   C7(♯5♭9♯11)

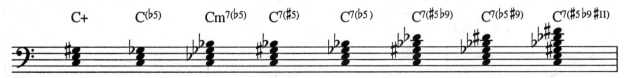

2 Octaves

C Altered

Cm⁷(♭5)

C♯ Altered

C♯m⁷(♭5)

D Altered

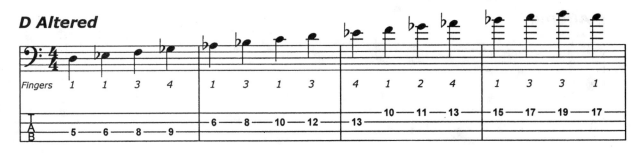

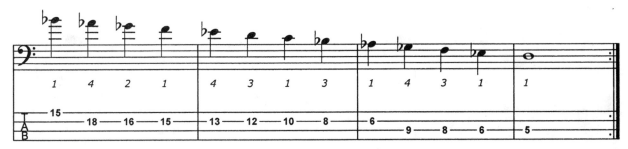

Dm⁷⁽♭⁵⁾

D♯ Altered

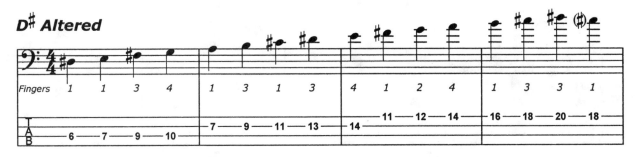

D♯m⁷⁽♭⁵⁾

2 Octaves

E Altered

Em7(♭5)

F Altered

Fm7(♭5)

F# Altered

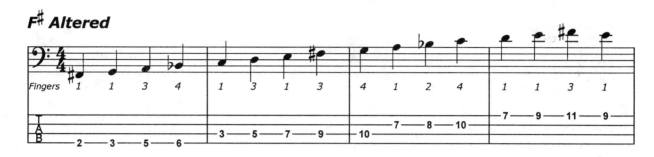

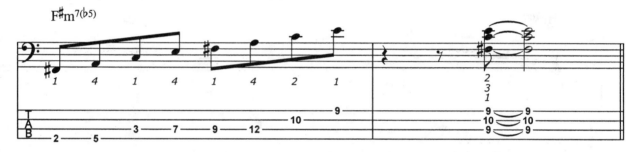

F#m7(b5)

G Altered

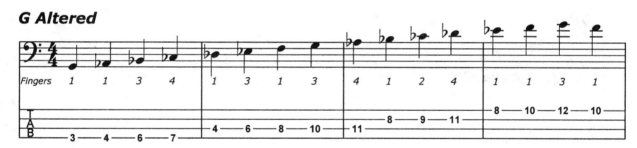

Gm7(b5)

69

G# Altered

A Altered

A# Altered

Fingers   1   1   3   4   1   3   1   3   4   1   2   4   1   3   3   1

1   4   2   1   4   3   1   3   1   4   3   1   1

A#m7(b5)

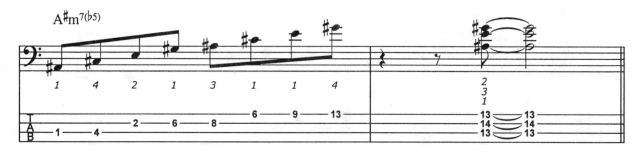

1   4   2   1   3   1   1   4   2 3 1

B Altered

Fingers   1   1   3   4   1   3   1   3   4   1   2   4   1   3   3   1

1   4   2   1   4   3   1   3   1   4   3   1   1

Bm7(b5)

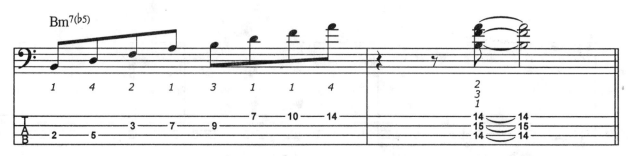

1   4   2   1   3   1   1   4   2 3 1

3 Octaves

B Altered

C Altered

D Altered

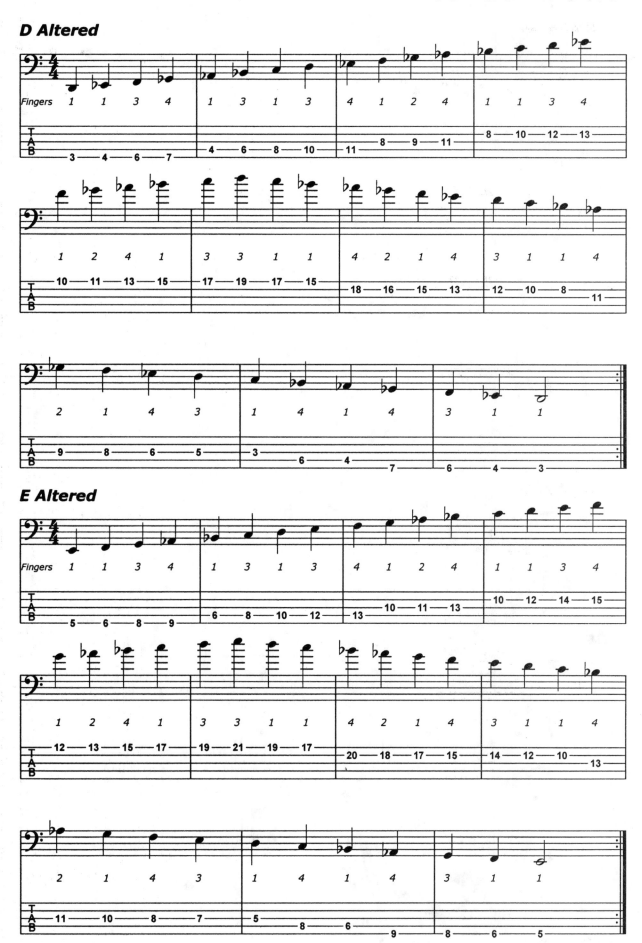

E Altered

The HARMONIC MINOR Scale

The Harmonic Minor Scale

W	H	W	W	H	W+H	H

Harmonic Minor scale

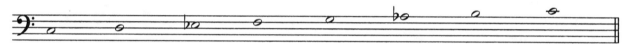

C Harmonic Minor (construction)

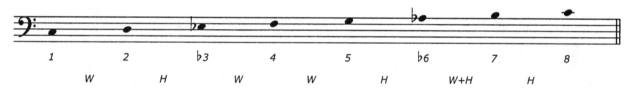

1	2	♭3	4	5	♭6	7	8
W	H	W	W	H	W+H	H	

One octave scale

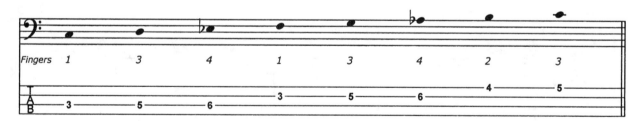

Chords

Cm   Cm(♭6)   Cm(add 9)   Cm(ma7)

2 Octaves

C Harmonic minor

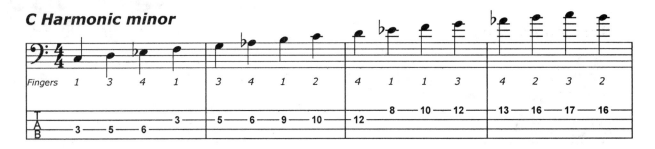

Fingers   1   3   4   1   3   4   1   2   4   1   1   3   4   2   3   2

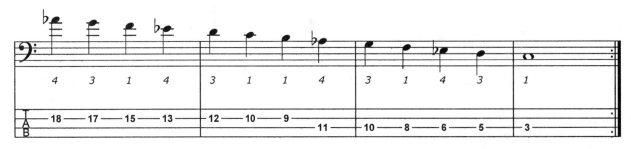

4   3   1   4   3   1   1   4   3   1   4   3   1

Cm(ma7)

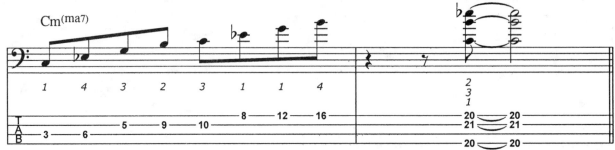

1   4   3   2   3   1   1   4   2
                                                 3
                                                 1

C# Harmonic minor

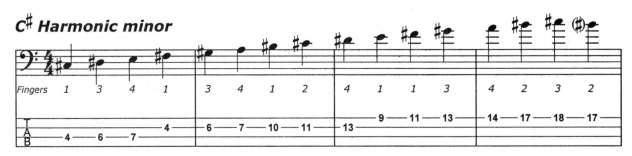

Fingers   1   3   4   1   3   4   1   2   4   1   1   3   4   2   3   2

4   3   1   4   3   1   1   4   3   1   4   3   1

C#m(ma7)

1   4   3   2   3   1   1   4   2
                                                 3
                                                 1

76

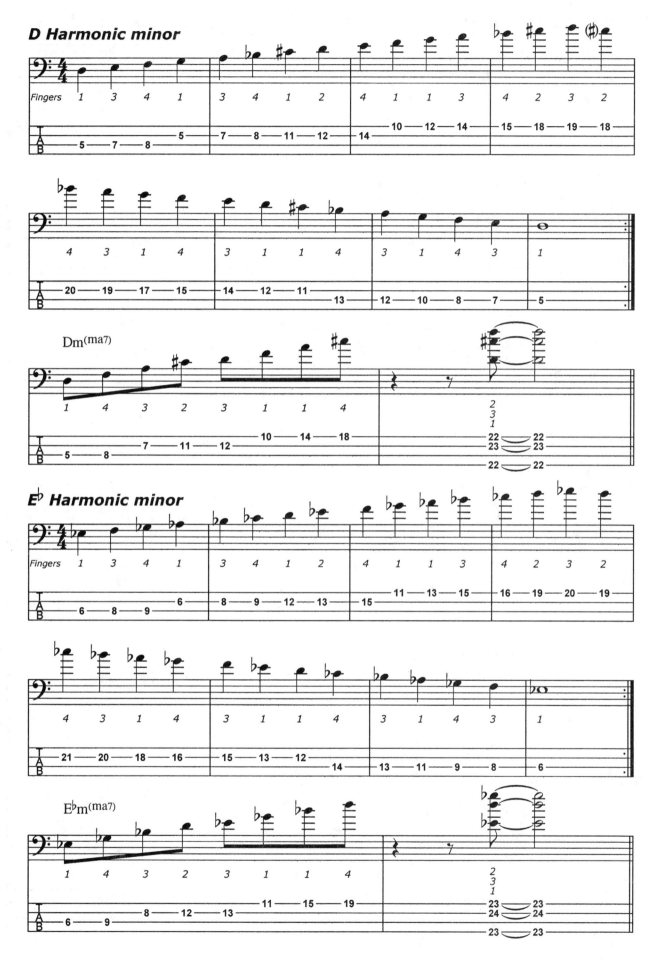

2 Octaves

E Harmonic minor

Em(ma7)

F Harmonic minor

Fm(ma7)

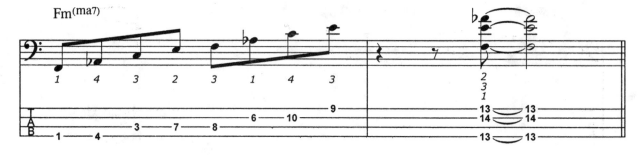

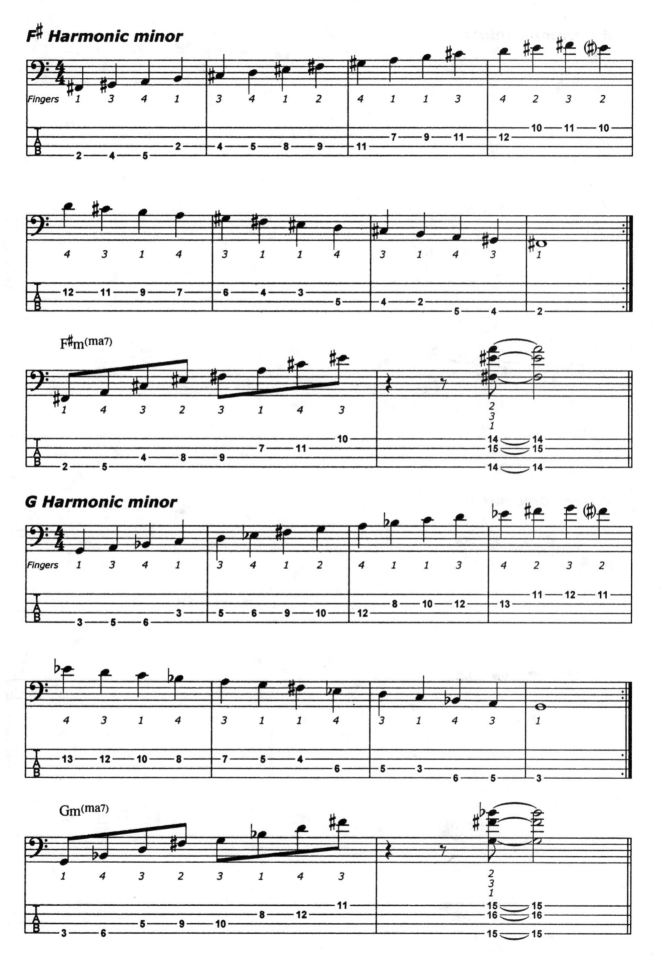

2 Octaves

A♭ Harmonic minor

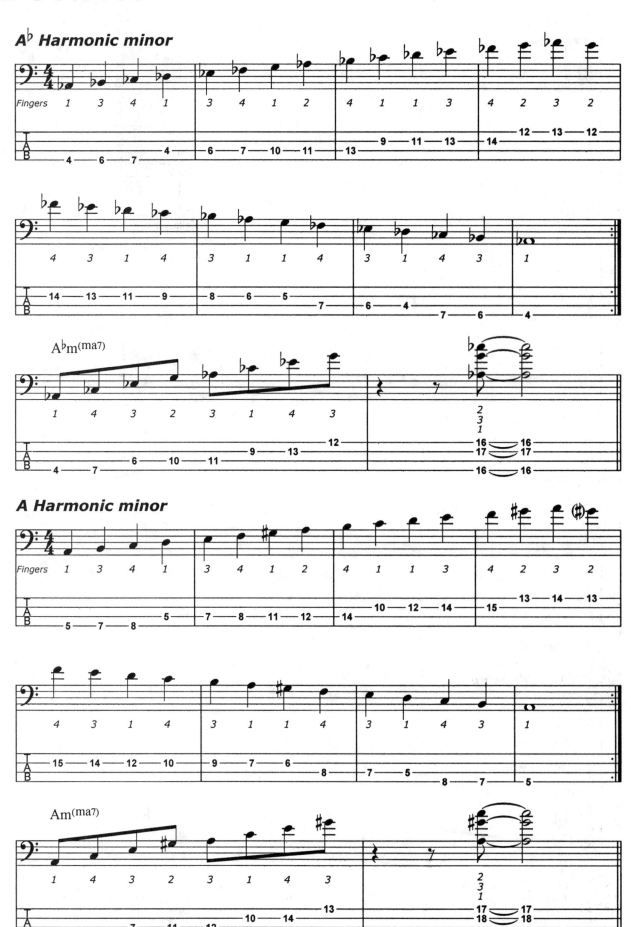

A Harmonic minor

B♭ Harmonic minor

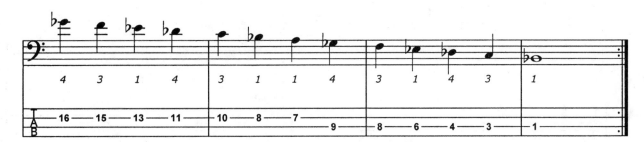

B Harmonic minor

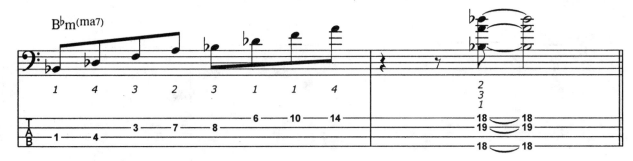

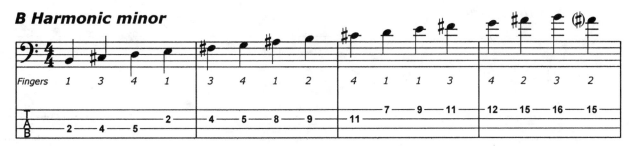

3 Octaves

B Harmonic Minor

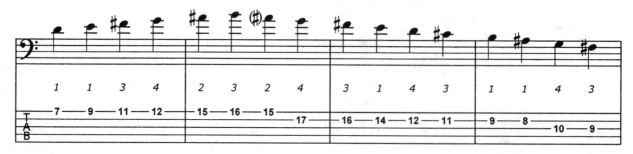

C Harmonic Minor

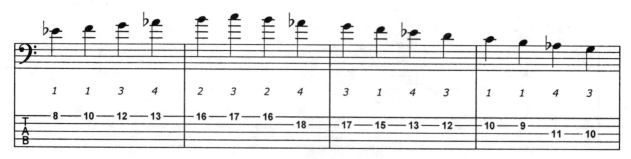

D Harmonic Minor

E Harmonic Minor

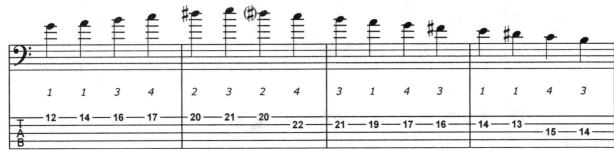

The DIMINISHED Scale

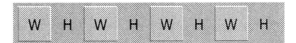

Diminished scale

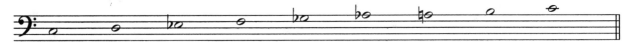

C Diminished (construction)

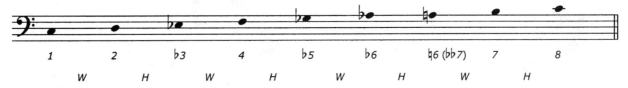

1	2	b3	4	b5	b6	♮6 (bb7)	7	8
W	H	W	H	W	H	W	H	

One octave scale

Chords

C°   C°7

2 Octaves

C Diminished

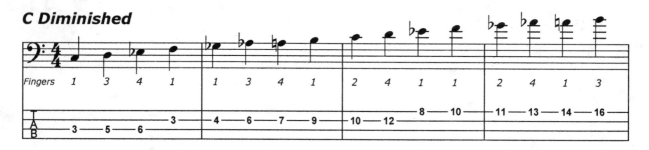

C# Diminished

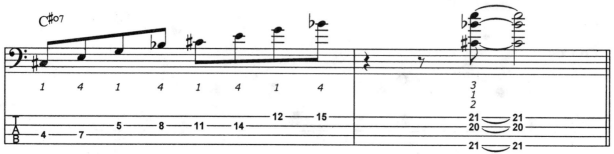

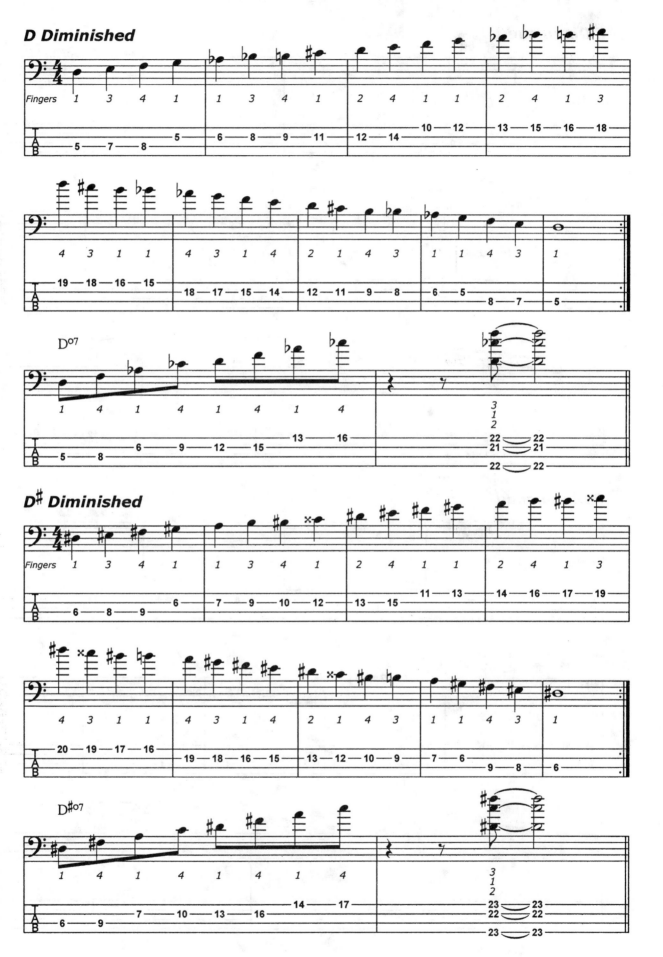

D Diminished

D°7

D# Diminished

D#°7

2 Octaves

E Diminished

E°7

F Diminished

F°7

88

F# Diminished

F#o7

G Diminished

Go7

2 Octaves

G# Diminished

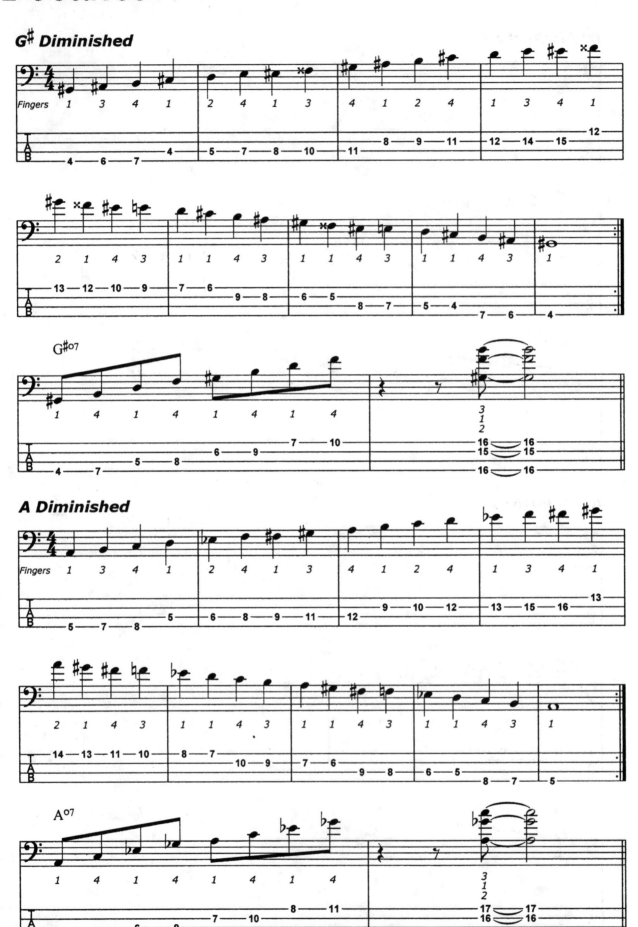

A Diminished

Bb Diminished

B Diminished

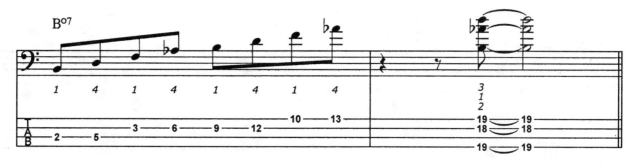

3 Octaves

B Diminished

C Diminished

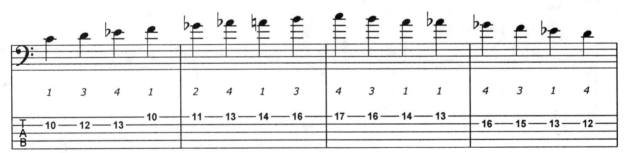

D Diminished

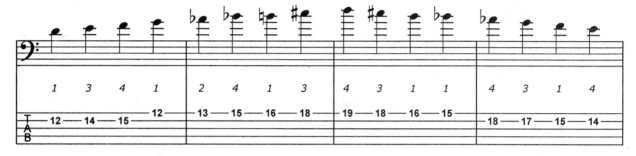

E Diminished

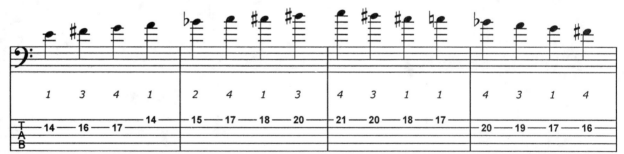

The DIMINISHED H/W Scale

The Diminished H/W Scale

Diminished Half/Whole scale

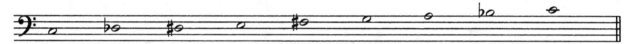

C Diminished H/W (construction)

One octave scale

Chords

2 Octaves

C Diminished H/W

D♭ Diminished H/W

D Diminished H/W

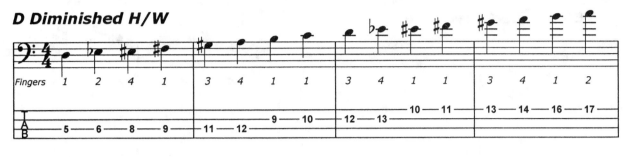

D⁷

E♭ Diminished H/W

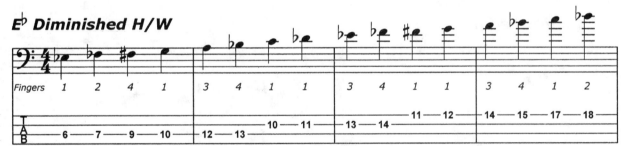

E♭⁷

2 Octaves

E Diminished H/W

E[7]

F Diminished H/W

F[7]

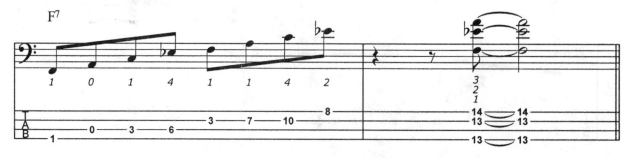

98

G♭ Diminished H/W

G Diminished H/W

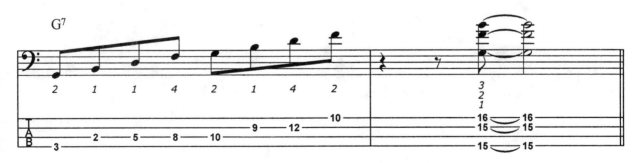

2 Octaves

A♭ Diminished H/W

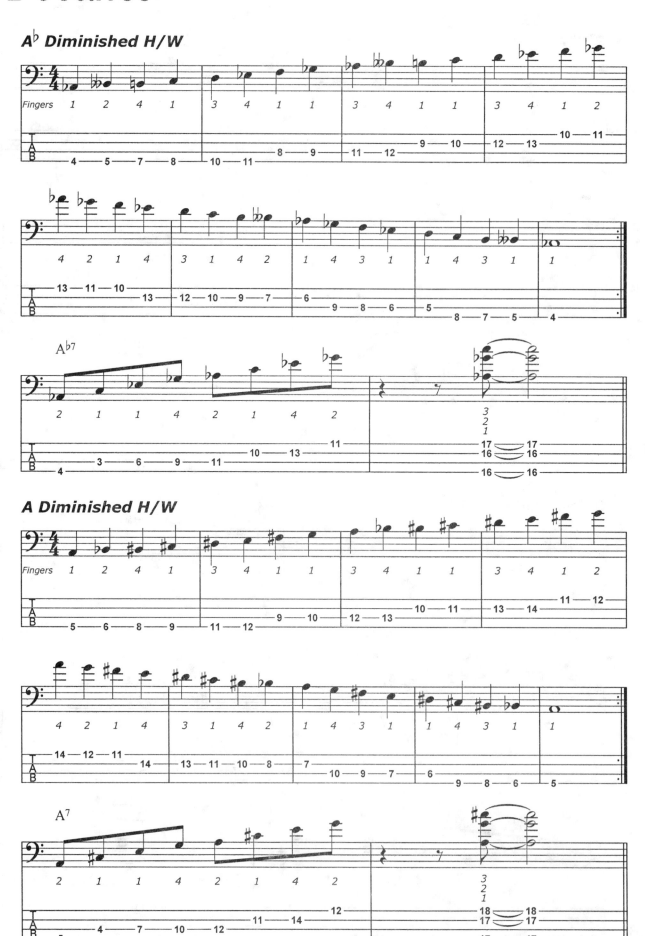

A Diminished H/W

100

B♭ Diminished H/W

B♭7

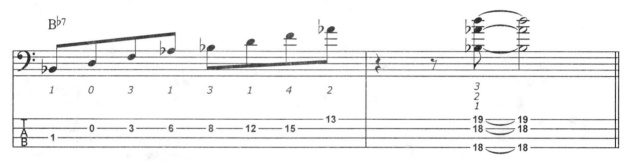

B Diminished H/W

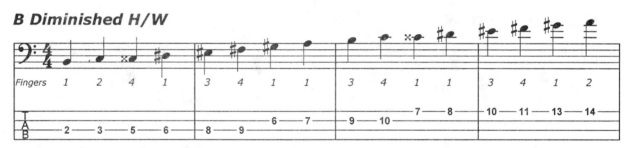

B7

3 Octaves

B Diminished H/W

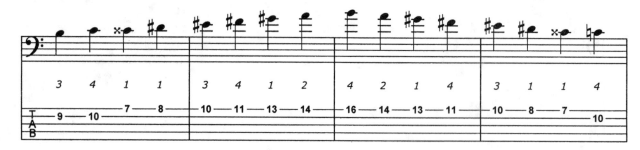

C Diminished H/W

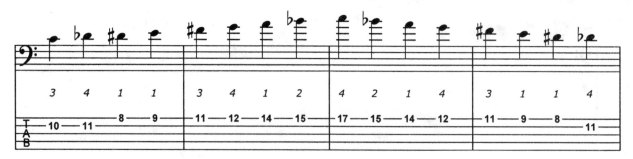

D Diminished H/W

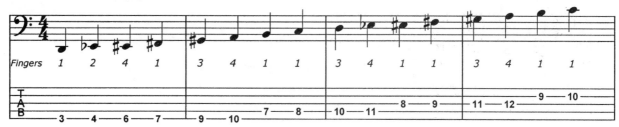

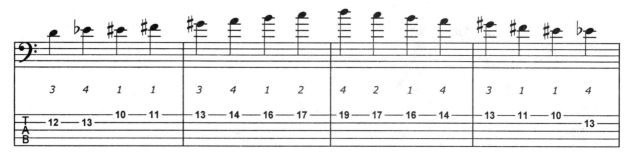

E Diminished H/W

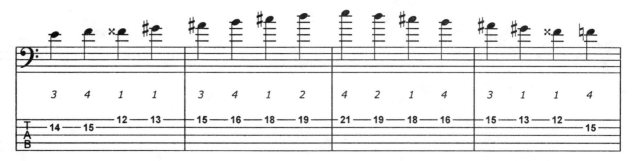

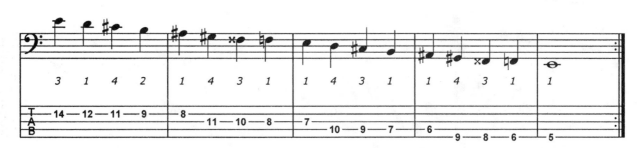

The WHOLE-TONE Scale

W W W W W W

Whole Tone scale

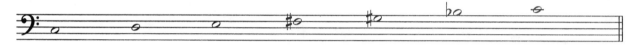

C Whole Tone (construction)

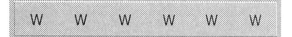

One octave scale

Chords

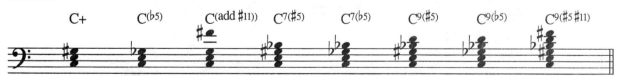

2 Octaves

C Whole Tone

D♭ Whole Tone

D Whole Tone

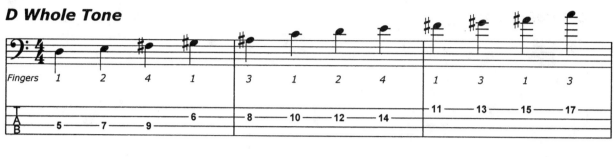

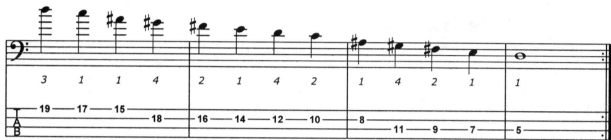

D7(#5)

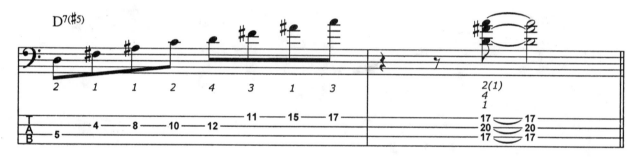

E♭ Whole Tone

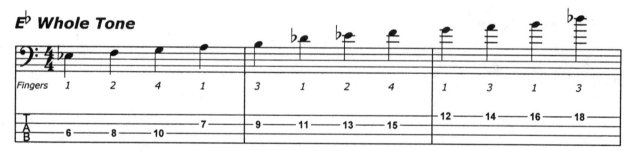

E♭7(#5)

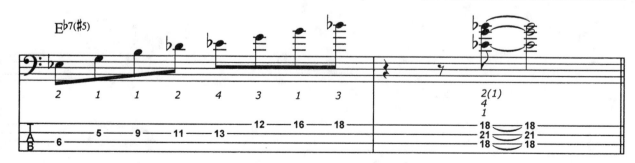

2 Octaves

E Whole Tone

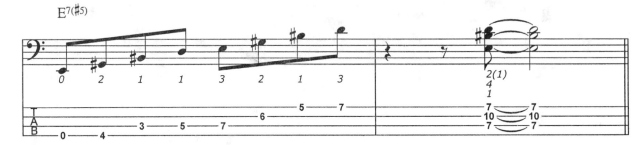

F Whole Tone

G♭ Whole Tone

G Whole Tone

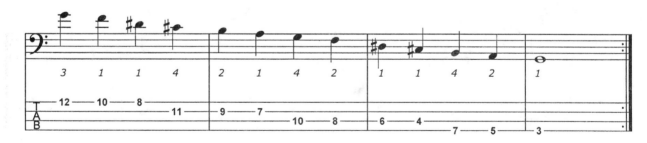

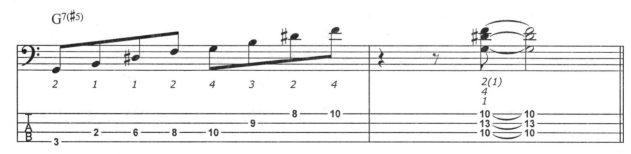

2 Octaves

A♭ Whole Tone

A♭7(♯5)

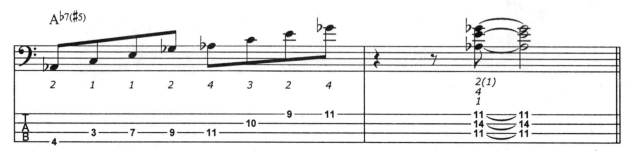

A Whole Tone

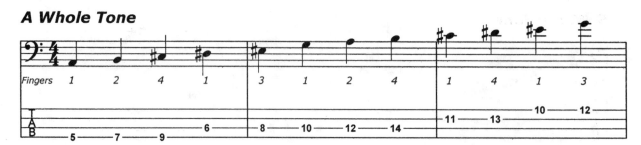

A7(♯5)

B♭ Whole Tone

B Whole Tone

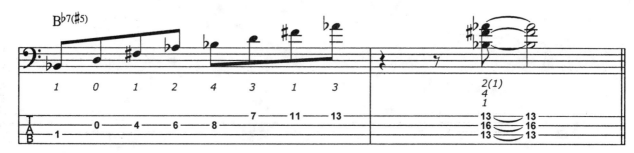

3 Octaves

B Whole Tone

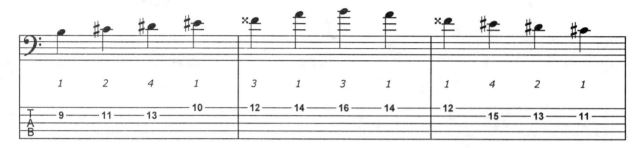

C Whole Tone

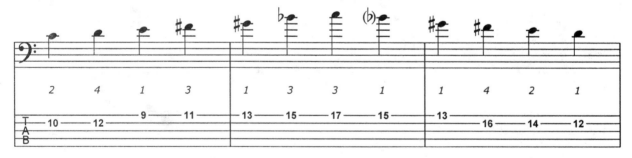

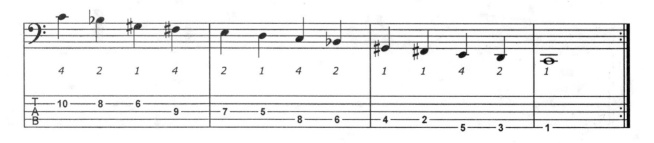

D Whole Tone

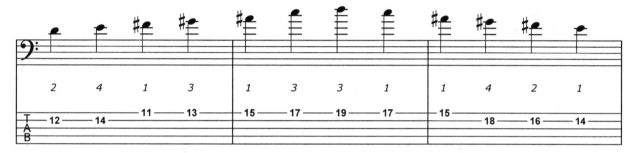

E Whole Tone

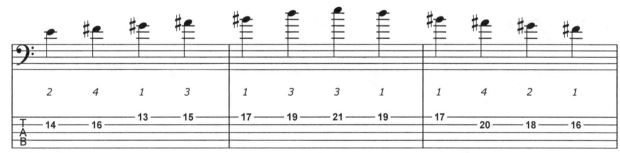

The BLUES Scale

The Blues Scale

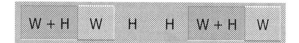

Blues scale

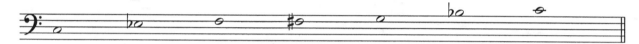

C Blues (scale construction)

One octave scale

Chords

2 Octaves

C Blues (scale)

Cm⁷

D♭ Blues

D♭m⁷

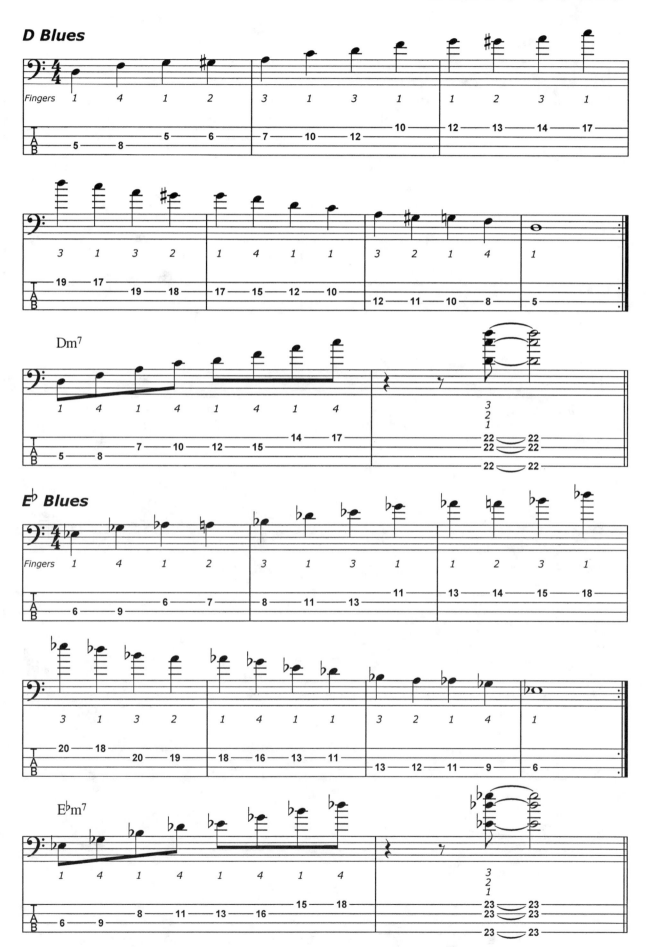

2 Octaves

E Blues

Em⁷

F Blues

Fm⁷

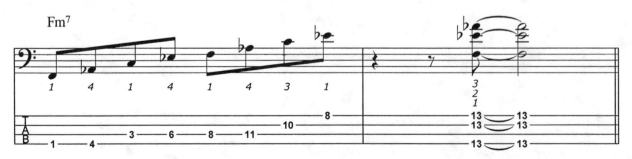

118

F# Blues

G Blues

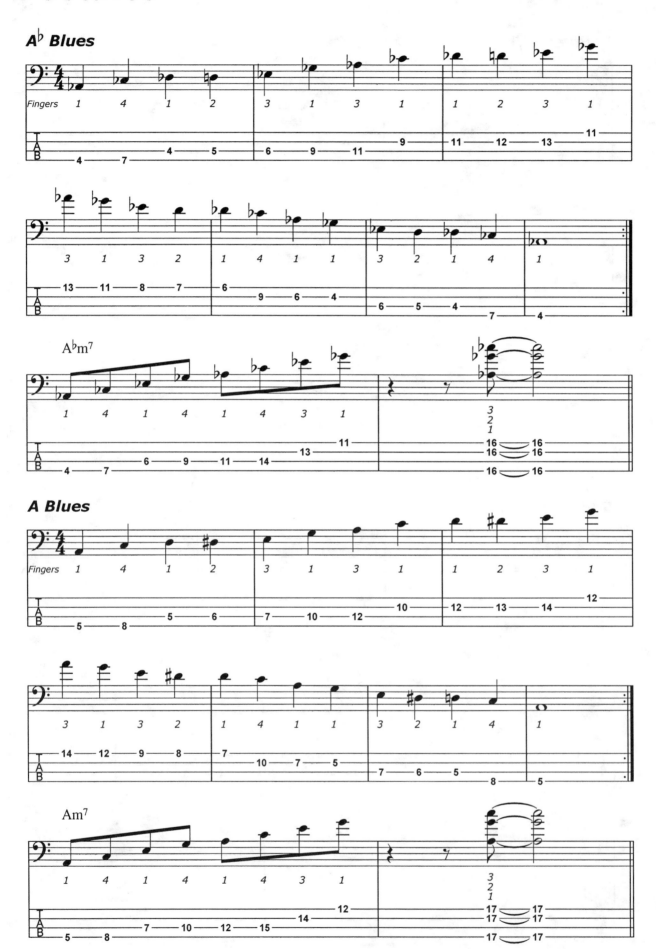

A♭ Blues

A♭m⁷

A Blues

Am⁷

B♭ Blues

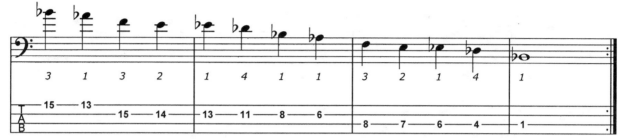

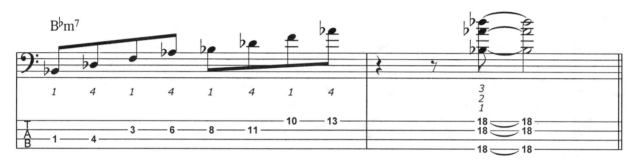

B Blues

3 Octaves

B Blues

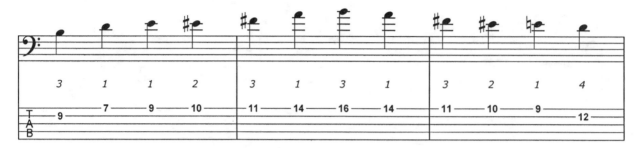

C Blues

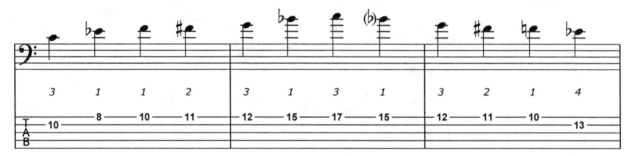

D Blues

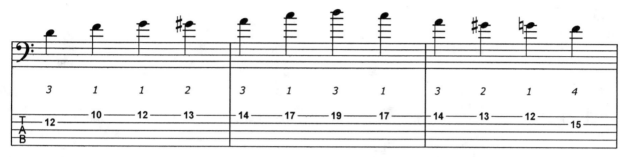

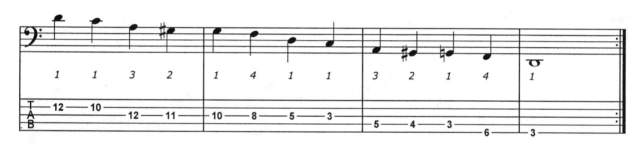

E Blues

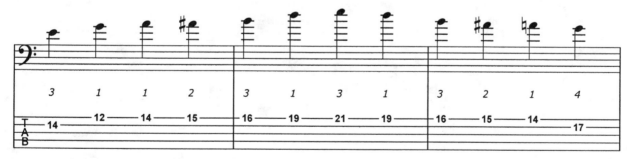

JUST Jazz REAL BOOK

250 Songs
Just Jazz Tunes and Jazz Standards
Just the "Right" Changes
Suggested Chord Substitutions
Lyrics Included
Composer Index
Complete Discography

The *Just Jazz Real Book* features 250 classic jazz tunes. These songs form the required core repertoire for all working jazz musicians.

500 MILES HIGH
A FELICIDADE
AIN'T MISBEHAVIN'
AIR CONDITIONING
AIREGIN
AJA
ALICE IN WONDERLAND
ALL MY TOMORROWS
ALL OR NOTHING AT ALL
ALL THE THINGS YOU ARE
ALONE TOGETHER
ANNA MARIA
ANTHROPOLOGY
ARMAGEDDON
AS TIME GOES BY
AU PRIVAVE
AUTUMN IN NEW YORK
AZURE
BE-BOP
BERNIE'S TUNE
BEYOND THE SEA
BIRD FEATHERS
BIRD'S NEST
BLACK NILE
BLACKBERRY WINTER
BLUE AND SENTIMENTAL
BLUE 'N' BOOGIE
BLUE RONDO A LA TURK
BLUE TRAIN
BLUES FOR ALICE
BLUESETTE
BODY AND SOUL
BONGO BOP
BONGO'S BEEP
BOPLICITY
BOULEVARD OF BROKEN DREAMS
BUT BEAUTIFUL
BYE BYE BLACKBIRD
C JAM BLUES
CANATALOUPE ISLAND
CARAVAN
CAST YOUR FATE TO THE WIND
CENTRAL PARK WEST
CHAMELEON
CHEGA DE SAUDADE
A CHILD IS BORN
CHRISTMAS TIME IS HERE
COME BACK TO ME
COME SUNDAY
CONFIRMATION
COOL BLUES
COTTON TAIL
COUNT DOWN
CRYSTAL SILENCE
CUTE
DAY IN THE LIFE OF A FOOL
DAYS OF WINE AND ROSES
DEACON BLUES
DESAFINADO
DEXTERITY
DIZZY ATMOSPHERE

DO IT AGAIN
DO NOTHIN' TILL YOU HEAR
 FROM ME
DOLPHIN DANCE
DONNA LEE
DON'T BLAME ME
DON'T EXPLAIN
DON'T GET AROUND MUCH
 ANYMORE
DRIFTING ON A REED
THE DUKE
EARLY AUTUMN
EASY TO LOVE
EMBRACEABLE YOU
EMILY
EPISTROPHY
ESP
EUROPA
EVERYTIME WE SAY GOODBYE
FALL
FALLING IN LOVE WITH LOVE
FASCINATIN' RHYTHM
A FINE ROMANCE
A FOGGY DAY
FOOTPRINTS
FOUR
FREEDOM JAZZ DANCE
GEE BABY, AIN'T I BEEN
 GOOD TO YOU
THE GENTLE RAIN
GIANT STEPS
THE GIRL FROM IPANEMA
GIRL TALK
GOOD BAIT
GOOD MORING, HEARTACHE
GROOVIN' HIGH
HAVE YOU MET MISS JONES
HERE'S THAT RAINY DAY
HIT THAT JIVE JACK
HONEYSUCKLE ROSE
HOT HOUSE
HOW HIGH THE MOON
HOW INSENSITIVE
HOW LONG HAS THIS
 BEEN GOING ON
I CAN'T GET STARTED
I COULD WRITE A BOOK
I DON'T STAND A GHOST OF
 A CHANCE WITH YOU
I GOT IT BAD (And That Ain't Good)
I GOT RHYTHM
I GOTTA RIGHT TO SING
 THE BLUES
I HEAR A RHAPSODY
I LET A SONG GO OUT
 OF MY HEART
I LOVE PARIS
I LOVE YOU
I MISS YOU
I SHOULD CARE
I'LL BE AROUND
I'LL REMEMBER APRIL
I'M AN ERRAND GIRL
 FOR RHTYHM
I'M BEGINNING TO SEE THE LIGHT
IMPRESSIONS
IN A MELLOW TONE
IN A SENTIMENTAL MOOD
IN WALKED BUD
IN YOUR OWN SWEET WAY

INVITATION
IS YOU IS OR IS YOU AIN'T
 (Ma Baby)
THE ISLAND
IT DON'T MEAN A THING
 (If It Ain't Got That Swing)
IT'S A RAGGY WALTZ
IT'S ONLY A PAPER MOON
I'VE GOT YOU UNDER MY SKIN
JAVA JIVE
JOSIE
JUST FRIENDS
KID CHARLEMAGNE
LA FIESTA
LADY SINGS THE BLUES
LAMP IS LOW (Pavane)
LAURA
LAZYBIRD
LESTER LEAPS IN
LI'L DARLIN'
LIMEHOUSE BLUES
LINUS AND LUCY
LITTLE AFRICAN FLOWER
 (Petite Fleur Africaine)
LITTLE BOAT
LOVE IS HERE TO STAY
LOVER MAN
LULLABY OF BIRDLAND
LUSH LIFE
MAIDEN VOYAGE
MAKIN' WHOOPIE
THE MAN I LOVE
MEDITATION
MINNIE THE MOOCHER
MISS OTIS REGRETS
MISTER FIVE BY FIVE
MISTY
MOMENT'S NOTICE
MOOD INDIGO
MOONLIGHT IN VERMONT
THE MORE I SEE YOU
MR. LUCKY
MR. PC
MY FOOLISH HEART
MY FUNNY VALENTINE
MY ROMANCE
MY SHIP
MYSTERIOUS TRAVELER
NAIMA
NATURE BOY
NEFERTITI
NIGHT AND DAY
A NIGHT IN TUNISIA
NIGHT TRAIN
OLD DEVIL MOON
OLEO
ON A CLEAR DAY
 (You Can See Forever)
ON GREEN DOLPHIN STREET
ONE NOTE SAMBA
OO SHOO BE DO BE
ORNITHOLOGY
OUR DELIGHT
OVER THE RAINBOW
PEG
PERDIDO
PETER GUNN
POINCIANNA
POLKA DOTS AND MOONBEAMS
PRELUDE TO A KISS

QUASIMODO
QUIET NIGHTS OF QUIET STARS
QUIET NOW
RELAXIN' AT CAMERILO
ROUND MIDNIGHT
SABIA
SALT PEANUTS
SATIN DOLL
SCRAPPLE FROM THE APPLE
SECRET LOVE
SKYLARK
SO NICE (Summer Samba)
SOLAR
SOLITUDE
SOME OTHER BLUES
SOME OTHER TIME
SOMEONE TO WATCH OVER ME
THE SONG IS YOU
SOPHISTICATED LADY
SPAIN
SPEAK LOW
SPRING CAN REALLY HANG
 YOU UP THE MOST
ST. THOMAS
STAIRWAY TO THE STARS
STAR EYES
STARDUST
STOMPIN' AT THE SAVOY
STRAIGHTEN UP AND FLY RIGHT
STREET OF DREAMS
STRUTTIN' WITH SOME BARBEQU
SUMMERTIME
SWEET GEORGIA BROWN
SWEET LORRAINE
TAIN'T NOBODY'S BUSINESS
 (If I Do)
TAKE FIVE
TEACH ME TONIGHT
TENOR MADNESS
THAT OLD FEELING
THEY CAN'T TAKE THAT
 AWAY FROM ME
THIS CAN'T BE LOVE
THIS MASQUERADE
TIME AFTER TIME
TIMES LIE
TONES FOR JOAN'S BONES
TUNE UP
TWISTED
VALSE HOT
WATCH WHAT HAPPENS
WATERMELON MAN
THE WAY YOU LOOK TONIGHT
WHILE WE'RE YOUNG
WILLOW WEEP FOR ME
WINDOWS
WITCH HUNT
YARDBIRD SUITE
YESTERDAYS
YOU MUST BELIEVE IN SPRING
YOU STEPPED OUT OF A DREAM
YOU'D BE SO NICE TO COME
 HOME TO
YOUNG AND FOOLISH
YOU'RE GETTING TO BE A
 HABIT WITH ME